MORE PICTURES ABOUT STOCKPORT IN CHESHIRE

A FURTHER COLLECTION OF PHOTOGRAPHS

BY

H. LEES

Published by
E. J. MORTEN (Publishers),
Didsbury, Manchester 20.
1971

First Published 1971
by E. J. Morten (Publishers),
Warburton Street, Didsbury, Manchester 20.

ISBN 0 901598 31 3 Paper
ISBN 0 901598 29 1 Cloth

Printed by The Acorn Press, Liverpool.

Youth looks at the building of a new Stockport.

FOREWORD

So much interest was shown in the first collection of Harry Lees' photographs that this follow-up, "More Pictures About Stockport", was demanded. These cover places such as The Heatons, Reddish, Offerton, Edgeley, and a host of other pictures of Stockport Centre omitted from "A Picture of Stockport" through lack of space.

Over the years Harry Lees has had the uncanny knack of photographing the unnoticed, bringing to light odd places and objects which have become so much a part of our everyday life that they remain unseen, yet when they are brought to our notice they take on a different view, sometimes humorous, sometimes depressing – but all of them, in their own way, holding a lot of nostalgic memories for the Stockport inhabitants.

We have endeavoured once again to give you another "Picture of Stockport" – a Stockport which is so quickly vanishing and being rebuilt at such a speed that only the shutter of a camera can keep it still.

There are well-known historical works about Stockport by authors such as Higginbotham, Earwaker and Ormerod but in "A Picture of Stockport" and this sequel "More Pictures about Stockport" the aim is to present a more personal view. Here you will see the house where you lived, the tramcar you rode on, the cinema you attended before the demolition squad moved in and the whole way of life began to change.

Harry Lees' pictures will be treasured as the years go by; his first book was very popular from the day of publication and is still in demand and I hope that this second collection of photographs will give just as much pleasure to Stockport people wherever they are living as well as the residents in the old town today.

E.J.M.

Left: Bennett's Iron Foundry, Green Lane, Heaton Norris,– erected 1906, demolished 1970. Allotments facing "Dig for Victory" in World War 1. Scene about mid-1920.

Above: Fleet of Cheshire Sterilised Milk waggons – the Dairy being erected in the early 1930's on the site of the old Green Lane allotments.

Right:
Warehouses and Heaton Norris Goods on Wellington Road North.

Lancashire Hill Council School,
known as "John Penny's,
closed August 1929.

Football team of "John Penny's", 1913.
(Mr. Thompson, Headmaster at the school.)

Terraced houses, Love Lane,
Heaton Norris, demolished in
1970's.

"Gardener's Arms", Old Road, Heaton Norris,
before demolition in 1960's.

Old Road, Heaton Norris, showing terraced
houses with cellar dwellings.

Hatton Street leading to Recreation Brow. Note the sign "Stockport County Supporters Club", also Corbishley's Pawn Shop with brass balls sign.

View looking over Lancashire Hill and Meadow Hill, Portwood, before demolition men started.

Lancashire Hill – shops, terraced houses and the Old "Nicholson Arms" before demolition.

View over Heaton Norris showing Manchester Road.

The new "Nicholson Arms", Penny Lane, with Hanover Flats towering above.

Terraced houses and courts in Penny Lane as it was in the 1950's.

A well-known lodging house for men in Bridgefield before 1960.

Top left:
"Vernon" Cinema, Carrington Road, closed in 1958.

Bottom left:
"Wellington" Cinema, Wellington Road South, closed in 1963 and turned into a Bingo Hall.

Bottom right:
"Alexandra" cinema, Castle Street, Edgeley; had talkies 1929, closed November 1961 and turned into supermarket.

Top right:
Programme of "Curzon" cinema, the opening in 1937 and closed 1960.

Close-up of Heaton Mersey Village,
in the foreground can be seen
the very narrow Heaton Place.

A delightful cobbled
approach to Vale Road,
Heaton Mersey.

Bird's eye view of Heaton Mersey.

Rear of Heaton Place.

Remains of old sewage works at Heaton Mersey.

Ring Mill Cotton Mill from the fields known locally as Railway Field.

A well-known figure with a love for horses in Reddish.

Left:
An old milk float, Mabens Milk, Canal Bank Farm, Reddish.

Above:
Transport: Steam at Reddish South Railway Station.

Old time horse-drawn furniture van on Waterloo Road, Houghton's.

Tandem and sidecar – an open-air sport in the 1920's and 1930's.

Coalmen loading coal on the Edgeley Railway sidings.

Heaton Mersey Village with its narrow road for traffic indicated on sign saying Heaton Place.

Travis Brook Mill, better known as McClure or Belgrave, later becoming Kingston No. 2.

Above:
Side of Portwood Mill, the Portwood Cut can be seen coming from the sluice gate.

Above: Remains of the old sluice gate before the Portwood Cut ran into the River Tame.
Below: Rear of Portwood Spinning Company. The old Portwood Cut can be seen.

Below:
View of Kingston Mill No. 1 Chestergate.

Skyline of Stockport. Clubhouse Hotel, Didsbury Road, houses on Huntsman Brow and modern flats of Hollywood, King Street and Mottram Street.

Heaton Norris skyline showing new industrial area and Heaton and Norris Towers flats.

Skyline looking to Edgeley and part of Huntsman Brow area.

Larkhill Brow. Known as "Spy and Cop" of Brinksway – leading to Edgeley.

Stockport Street, in Hope Hill District. Terraced houses, demolished early 1970.

Brinksway.
Terraced houses on the main road to Cheadle.

Looking down on 'Brinksway', called the "Rocks". Ring Mills Cotton Mill can be seen.

On the banks of the River Mersey. These caves could be seen in the 1950's.

Right:
Walthew's Cotton Mill, bottom shop on the Banks of the River Mersey, Brinksway.

Below left:
A close-up view of the Pledge Office where transactions took place.

Below right:
Chestergate with "Motts Pawnbrokers" standing at corner of street.

Close-up of Heaton Mersey Village,
in the foreground can be seen
the very narrow Heaton Place.

A delightful cobbled
approach to Vale Road,
Heaton Mersey.

Bird's eye view of Heaton Mersey.

Rear of Heaton Place.

Remains of old sewage works at Heaton Mersey.

Ring Mill Cotton Mill from the fields known locally as Railway Field.

A well-known figure with a love for horses in Reddish.

Left:
An old milk float, Mabens Milk, Canal Bank Farm, Reddish.

Above:
Transport: Steam at Reddish South Railway Station.

Old time horse-drawn furniture van on Waterloo Road, Houghton's.

Tandem and sidecar – an open-air sport in the 1920's and 1930's.

Coalmen loading coal on the Edgeley Railway sidings.

Heaton Mersey Village with its narrow road for traffic indicated on sign saying Heaton Place.

Travis Brook Mill, better known as McClure or Belgrave, later becoming Kingston No. 2.

Above:
Side of Portwood Mill, the Portwood Cut can be seen coming from the sluice gate.

Above: Remains of the old sluice gate before the Portwood Cut ran into the River Tame.
Below: Rear of Portwood Spinning Company. The old Portwood Cut can be seen.

Below:
View of Kingston Mill No. 1 Chestergate.

Skyline of Stockport. Clubhouse Hotel, Didsbury Road, houses on Huntsman Brow and modern flats of Hollywood, King Street and Mottram Street.

Heaton Norris skyline showing new industrial area and Heaton and Norris Towers flats.

Skyline looking to Edgeley and part of Huntsman Brow area.

Larkhill Brow. Known as "Spy and Cop" of Brinksway – leading to Edgeley.

Stockport Street, in Hope Hill District. Terraced houses, demolished early 1970.

Brinksway.
Terraced houses on the main road to Cheadle.

Looking down on 'Brinksway', called the "Rocks". Ring Mills Cotton Mill can be seen.

On the banks of the River Mersey. These caves could be seen in the 1950's.

Right:
Walthew's Cotton Mill, bottom shop on the Banks of the River Mersey, Brinksway.

Below left:
A close-up view of the Pledge Office where transactions took place.

Below right:
Chestergate with "Motts Pawnbrokers" standing at corner of street.

Where Banks Lane meets Hall St., standing on the corner is Union Chapel.

More steps leading from Underbank to St. Petersgate. Turners' Vaults or Queens Arms at the side.

"Goberg Steps" from the Market, dropping into Underbank, closed in the early 1960's.

Wellington Road South, corner of Hillgate, during War years: special police on duty.

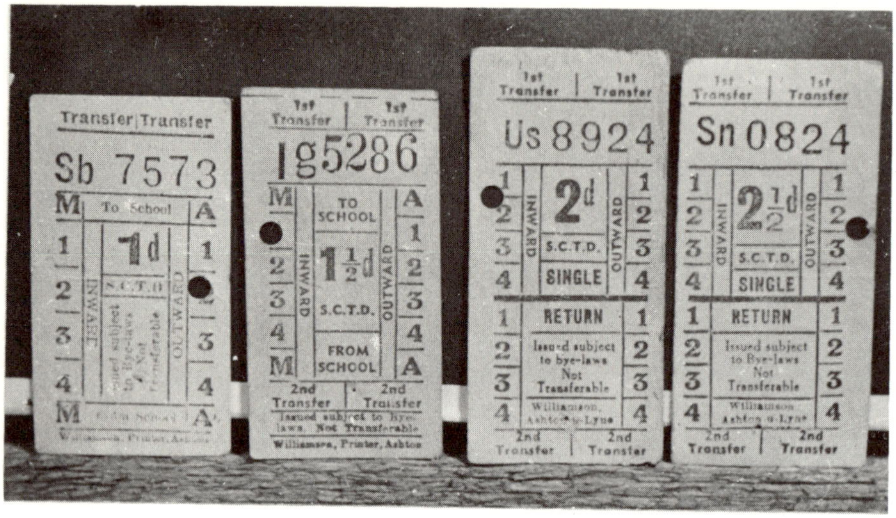

Tram tickets, Stockport Corporation.

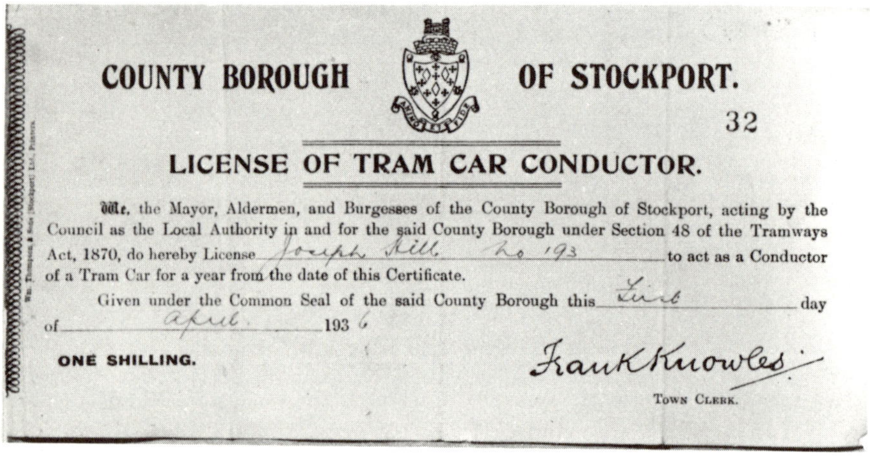

COUNTY BOROUGH OF STOCKPORT.

32

LICENSE OF TRAM CAR CONDUCTOR.

We, the Mayor, Aldermen, and Burgesses of the County Borough of Stockport, acting by the Council as the Local Authority in and for the said County Borough under Section 48 of the Tramways Act, 1870, do hereby License *Joseph Hill No 193* to act as a Conductor of a Tram Car for a year from the date of this Certificate.

Given under the Common Seal of the said County Borough this *First* day of *April* 193*6*

ONE SHILLING.

Frank Knowles

TOWN CLERK.

Licence of Stockport Tram Conductor, 1932.

Last sign, red and white letters on the Tiviot Dale Station, before closing.

Left:
Canal in Heaton Norris, Rivetts Cotton Mill, later becoming Cheadle Condensor Works: the warm water was a great attraction for young swimmers. The Canal was closed in 1962.

Below:
Railway Iron Bridge over the Canal about 1958.

Above:
Reddish Canal, known as Manchester and Ashton Canal. In the background is "Hallidays" Bankfield Dyeworks, demolished in the early 1960's.

Right:
Broadstone Mill cotton mill. In the foreground can be seen Kays' Chemical Works.

Waterloo Road, Hillgate: milkman delivering milk and sign advertising the "Star" cinema.

Bird's eye view of the Canal and Broadstone Road, Reddish, and council houses.

Broadstone Mill, Reddish, with its two chimneys and now called Broadstone House.

Market stalls in slack period.

Open-air stalls, Saturday afternoon 1970.

Market Place on a Sunday morning, early 1960.

Above:
Stockport Market in the early 1900's.

Left:
Shawcross Fold, Market Place: some warehouses of Grimsby Fish in the 1960's.

Below:
A well-known firm in Reddish "Greenhalgh's", noted in the 1920's for its marmalade in stone jars.

Left:
Canal Bank Farm, Broadstone Road.
Farmed by Mr. Maben.

Right:
Haymaking. Farmer Mr. Humphries of Church Farm and his men at work.

Below:
Reddish was well-known for farming. On the land with two horses, on fields where now stands C.W.S. Preserve Works.

"Joules Court", Hillgate, with flat-top horse carts.

Black and white building on Broadstone Hall Road South, built for Chairman Tobacco in the 1920's; later used by the C.W.S. as a Laundry, finally by Becks Transport, being demolished in January, 1968.

Greengrocer Mr. Sweet hawking his goods on Reddish Road in the 1960's.

Millstone Hotel, Lancashire Hill – and a bus coming out of Sandy Lane.

Edgeley Methodist Church, before demolition in June, 1969, to make way for the Precinct.

Whitehill House, sold by P. Newton by auction to Stockport Corporation in 1898 for an Isolation Hospital, later used for Civil Defence and flats before demolition in early 1960's.

More memories – Mersey Square, early 1900.

High Street, with cars
parking in the 1930's.

St. Stephen's Church, Ridgeway Lane,
in 1960, before demolition in 1962.

"Closing Down" ready for
demolition in Merseyway,
early 1960's.

Demolition,
Heaton Norris, 1971.

Castle Street, taken about 1960.

Castle Street, 1971.

Flats at Edgeley.

The Precinct, Edgeley, 1971.

View from Edgeley showing the flats at Hollywood.

Flats at Brinnington, taken from the footpath to Reddish Vale.

Well-known beauty spot. "Cromwells' Castle" or Ardern Hall, Bredbury.

Churchgate, the Black and White "Thatched Hotel" and three-story houses in the foreground.

Corbishley's Pawnshop, Hatton Street, Bridgefield: one of the last Pawnshops which was demolished in the early 1960's.

Heaton Lane with chimney sweep's brush coming out of chimney in late 1950's.

Newton's Whim, a quaint street
in Bridgefield.

A night view taken from
the Rock Steps, Bridgefield.

Two views of old Lancashire Hill in 1962.

Row of shops, Love Lane, Heaton Norris; awaiting demolition, 1971.

"Savoy" Cinema, Heaton Moor Road, March 1970, showing 'David Copperfield'. Cinema has now been modernised.

A sunny day on Heaton Moor Road with its trees in full bloom.

Heaton Chapel Station and the little lock-up shops nearby.

Shops on Heaton Moor Road with verandas.

More shops on Heaton Moor Road before alterations took place.

Bird's eye view of Stockport from Mottram Street Flats.